A FUNNY SWEAR WORD ADULT COLORING BOOK

We all have our favorite cuss words on hand for stubbed toes, moments of bewilderment and emphatic exclamations.

Shake up conversations, expand your vocabulary and elevate your language with these 40 swear-word alternatives desings sure to leave you and your listeners with the giggles rather than in shock

Each page is single-sided for getting the best Coloring Experience.

THIS COLORING BOOK BELONGS TO:

COLOR TEST PAGE

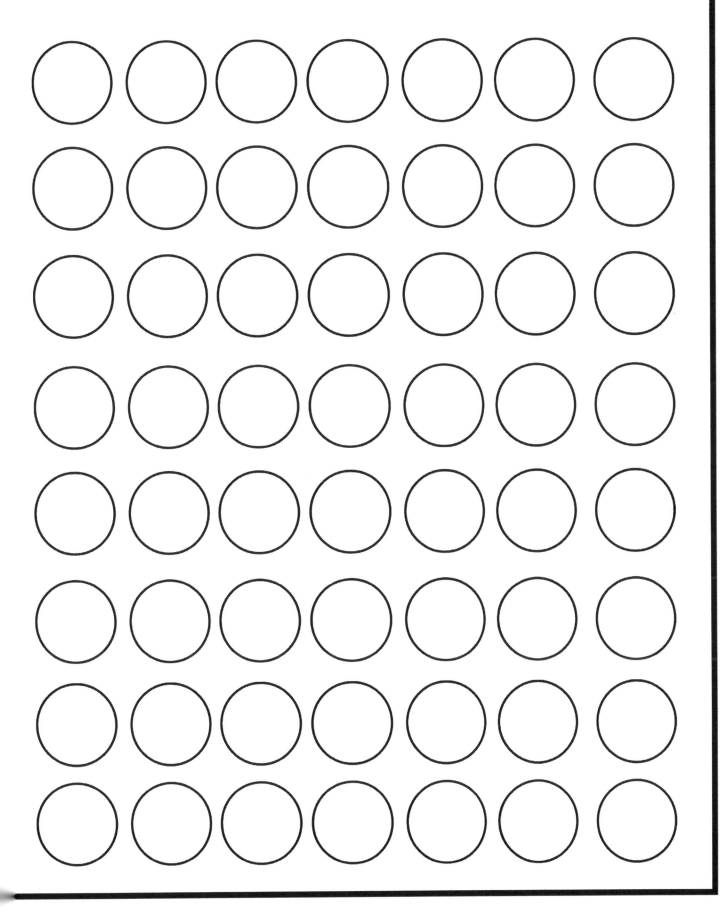

BSM CUSCOLO. Publising

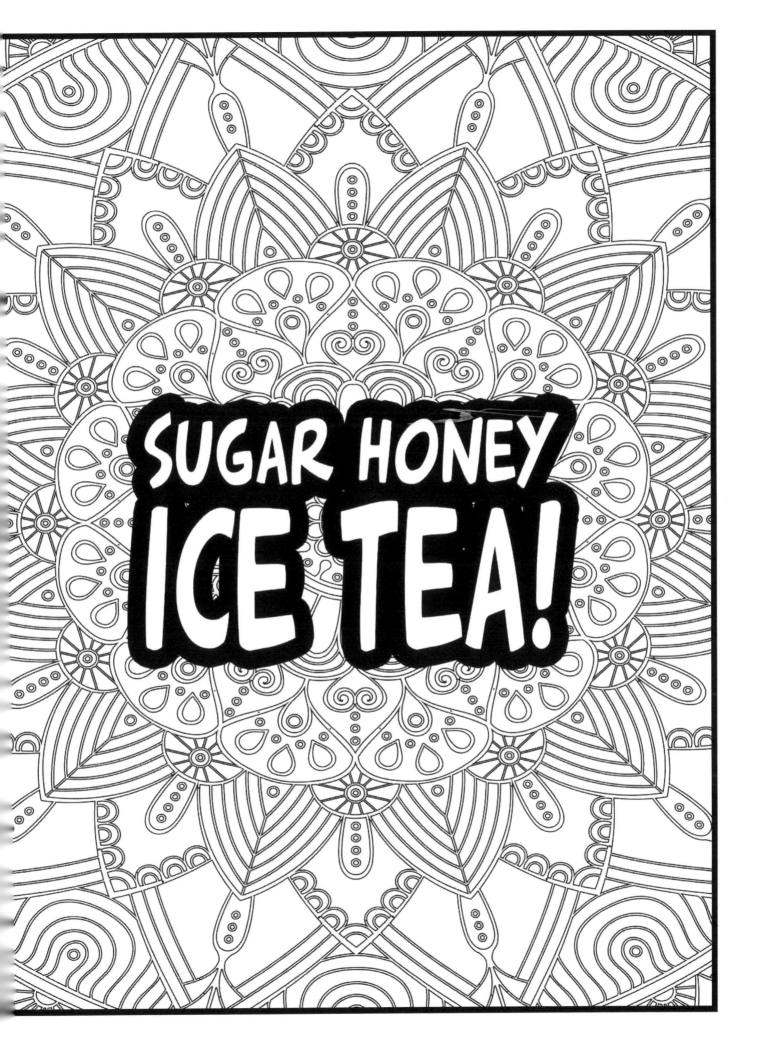

BSM CUSCOLO.
Publising

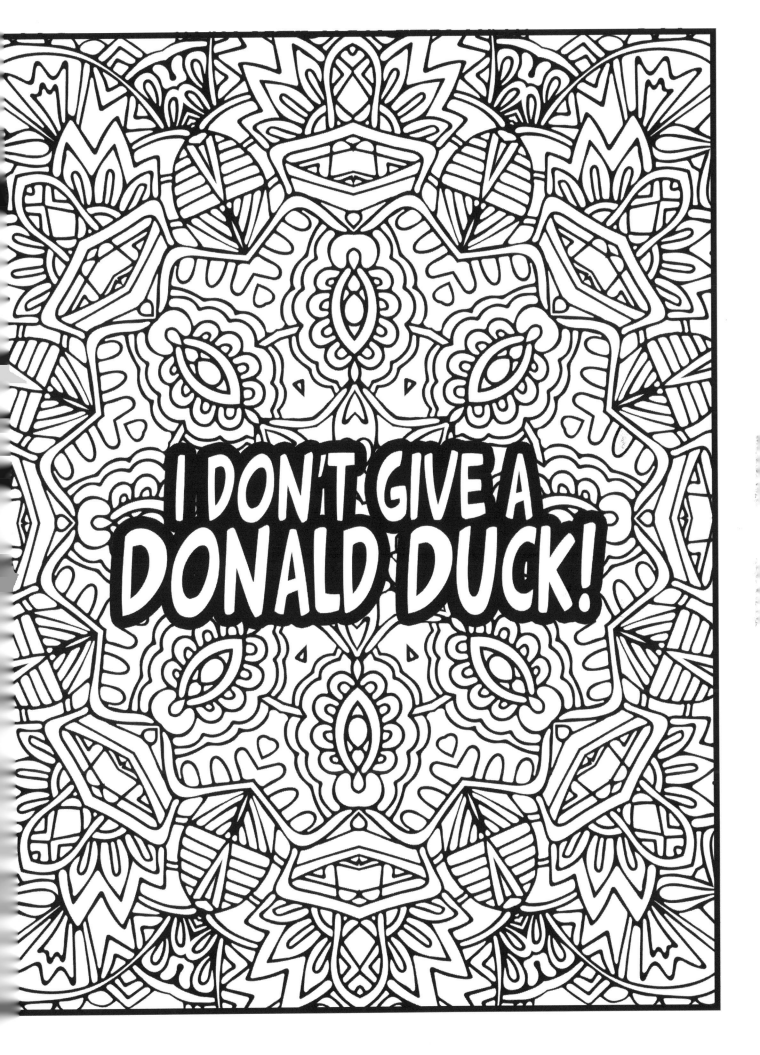

BSM CUSCOLO.
Publising

BSM CUSCOLO.
Publising

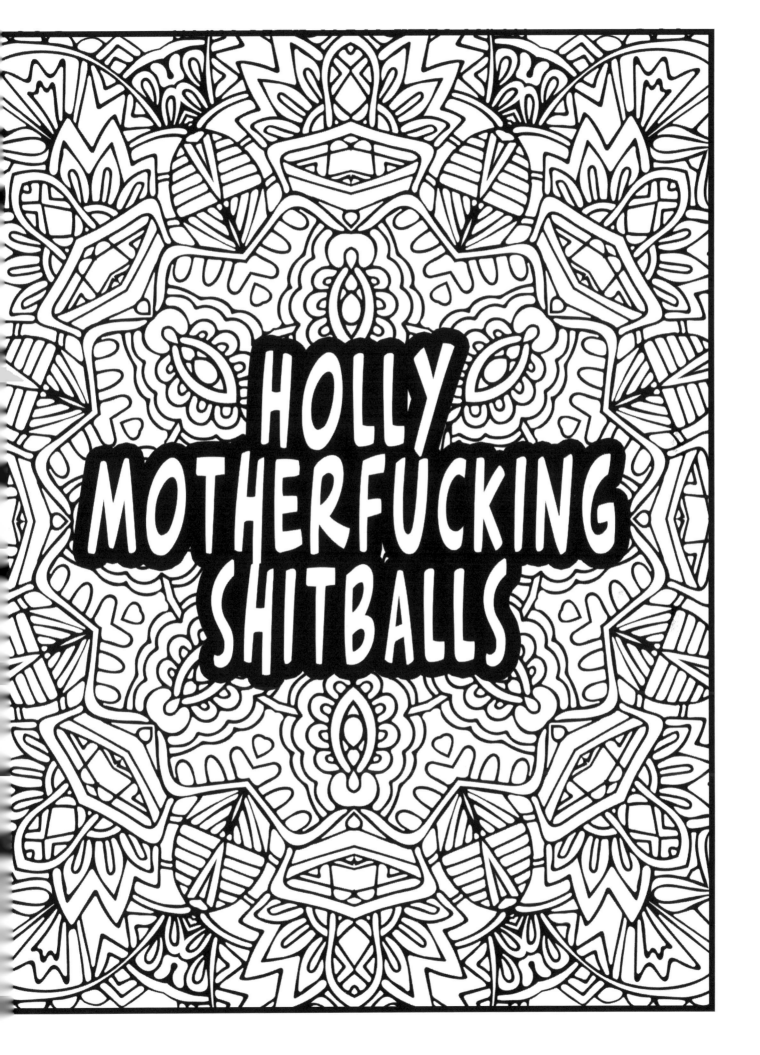

BSM CUSCOLO. Publising

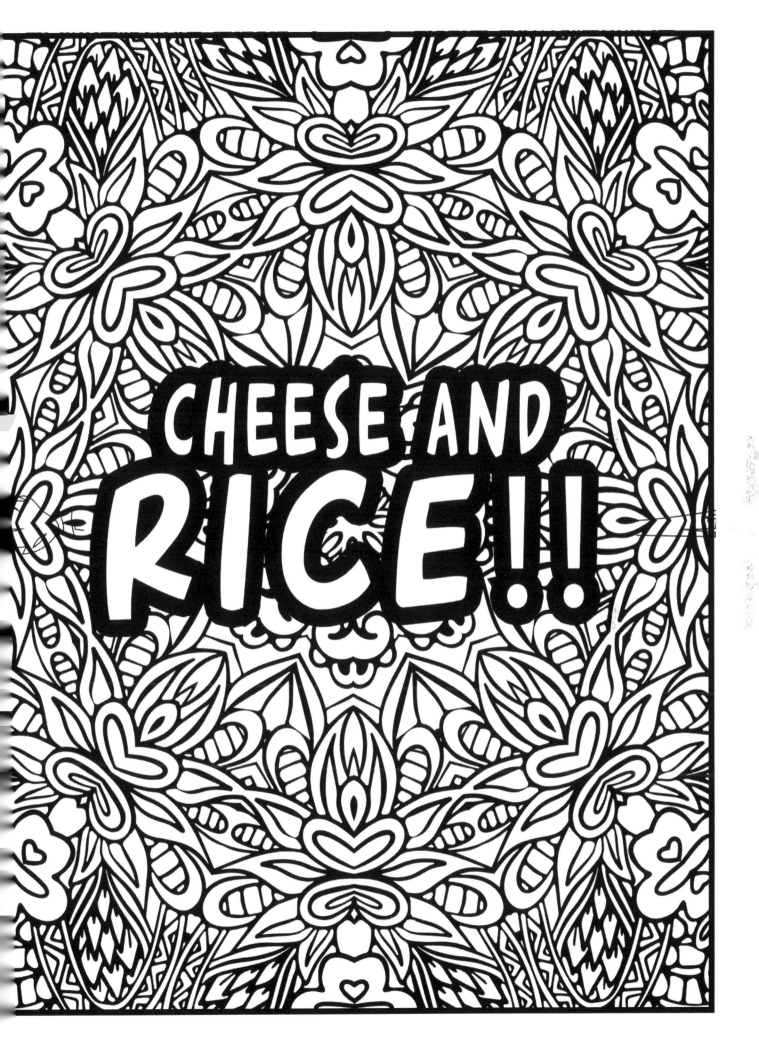

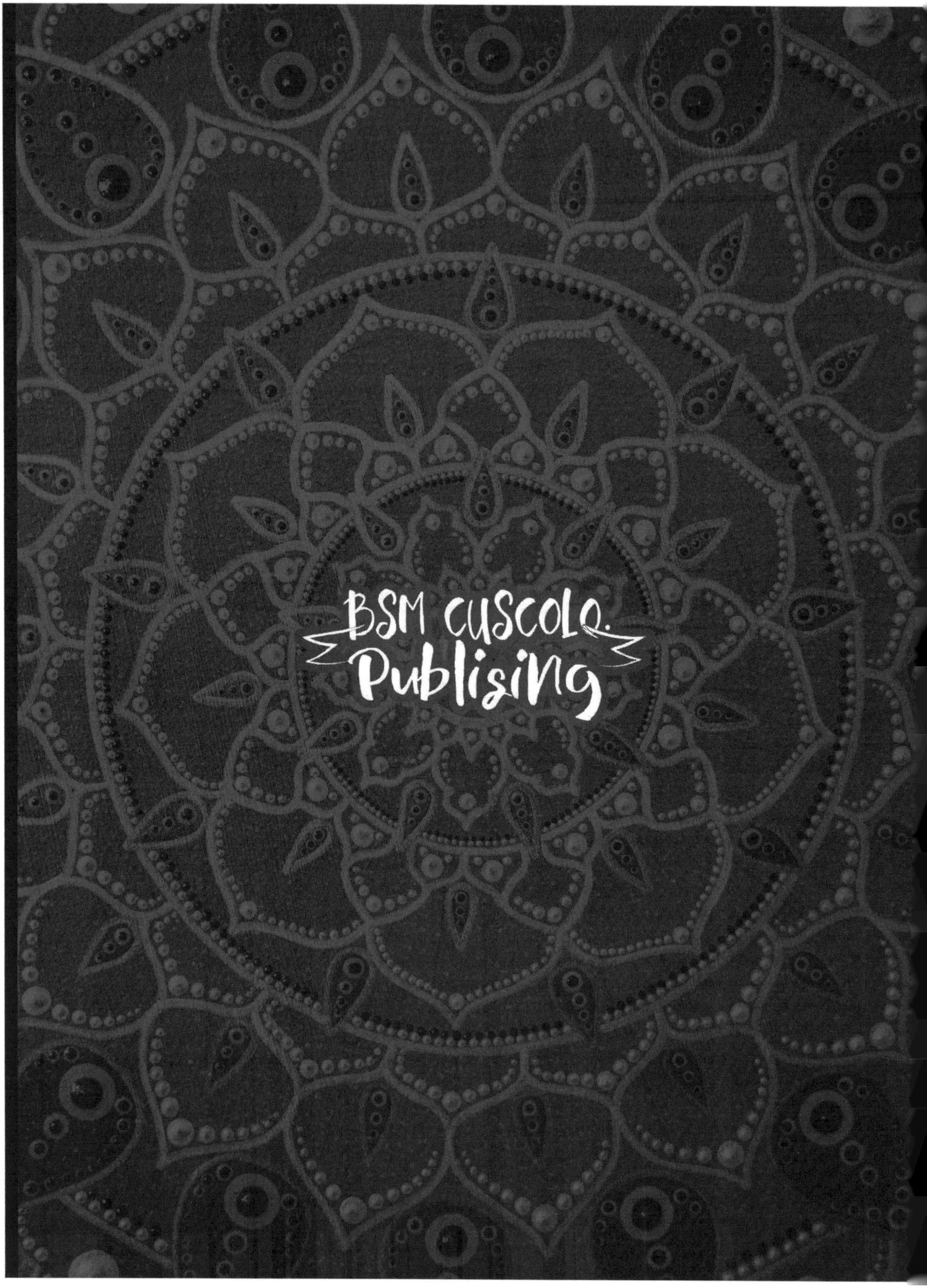
BSM CUSCOLE
Publising

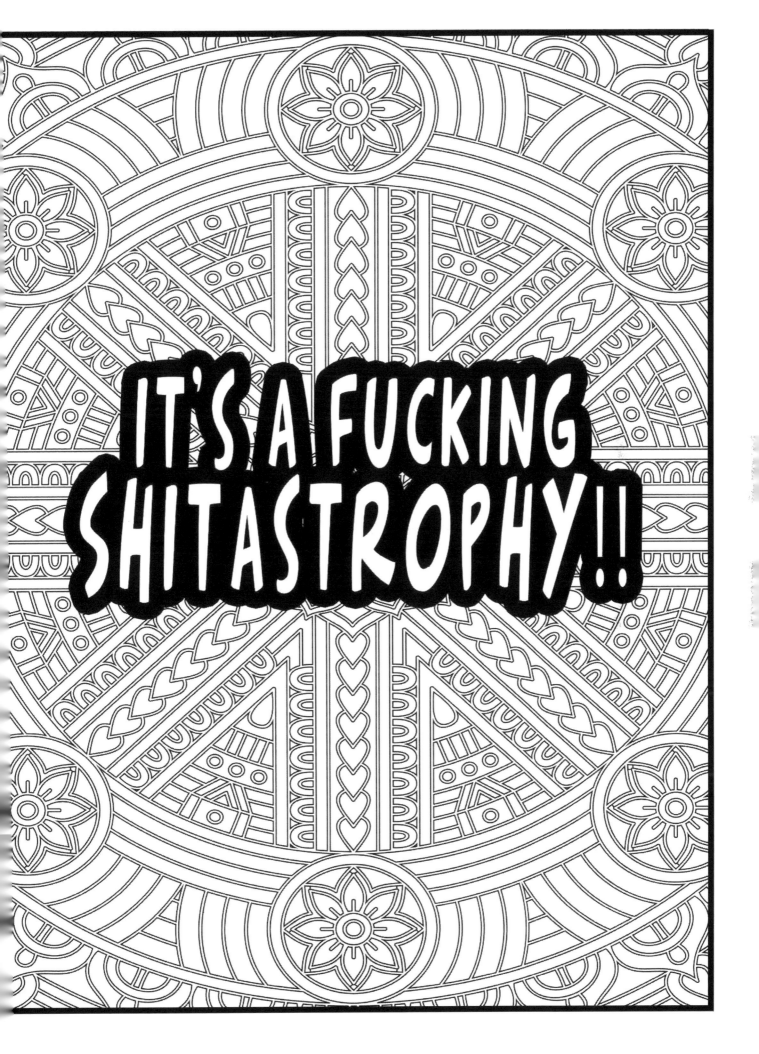

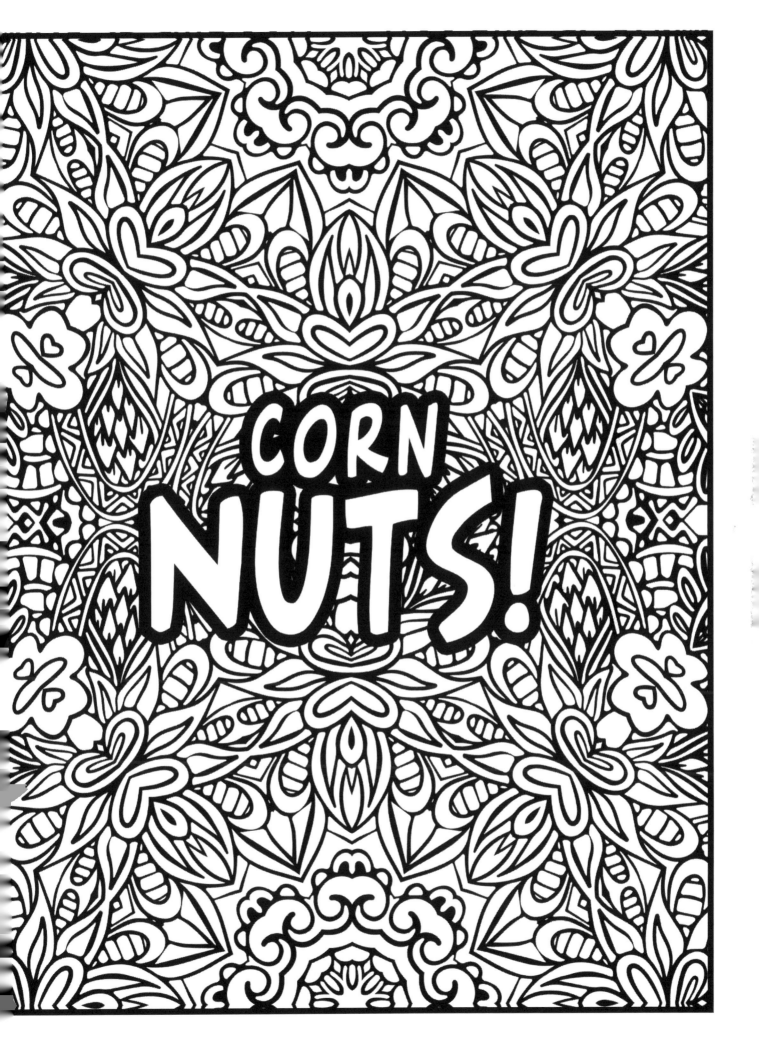

BSM CUSCOLO.
Publising

BSM CUSCOLO. Publising

BSM CUSCOLO.
Publising

BSM CUSCOLO.
Publising

BSM CUSCOLO. Publising

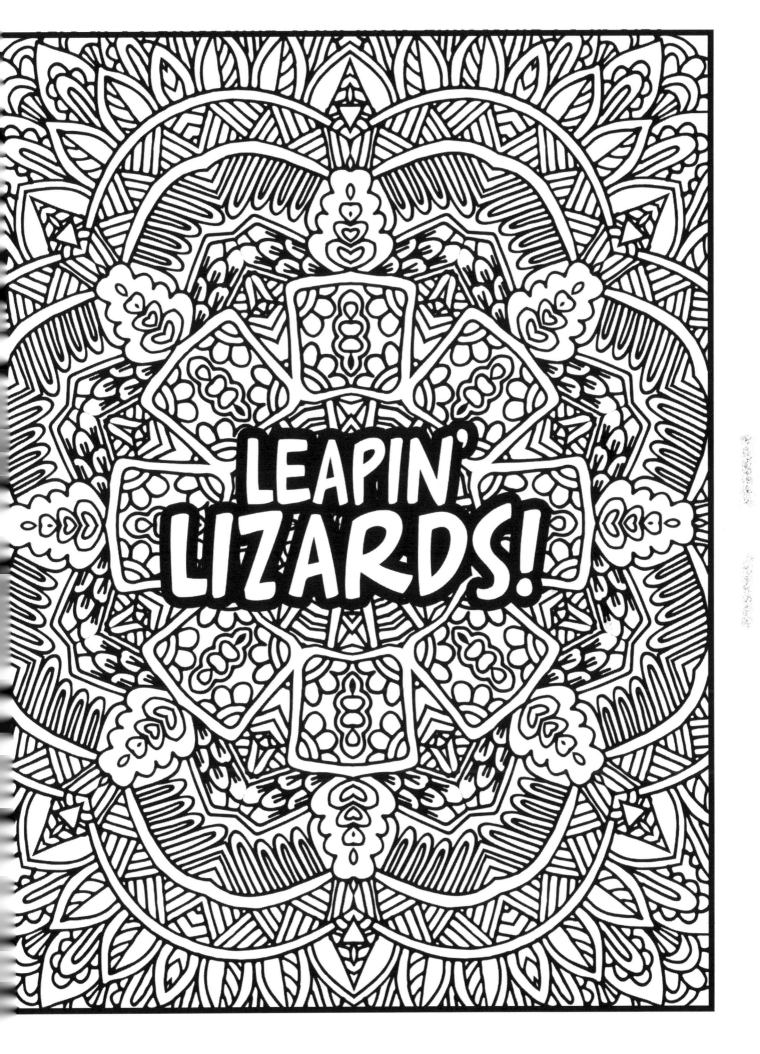

BSM CUSCOLO.
Publising

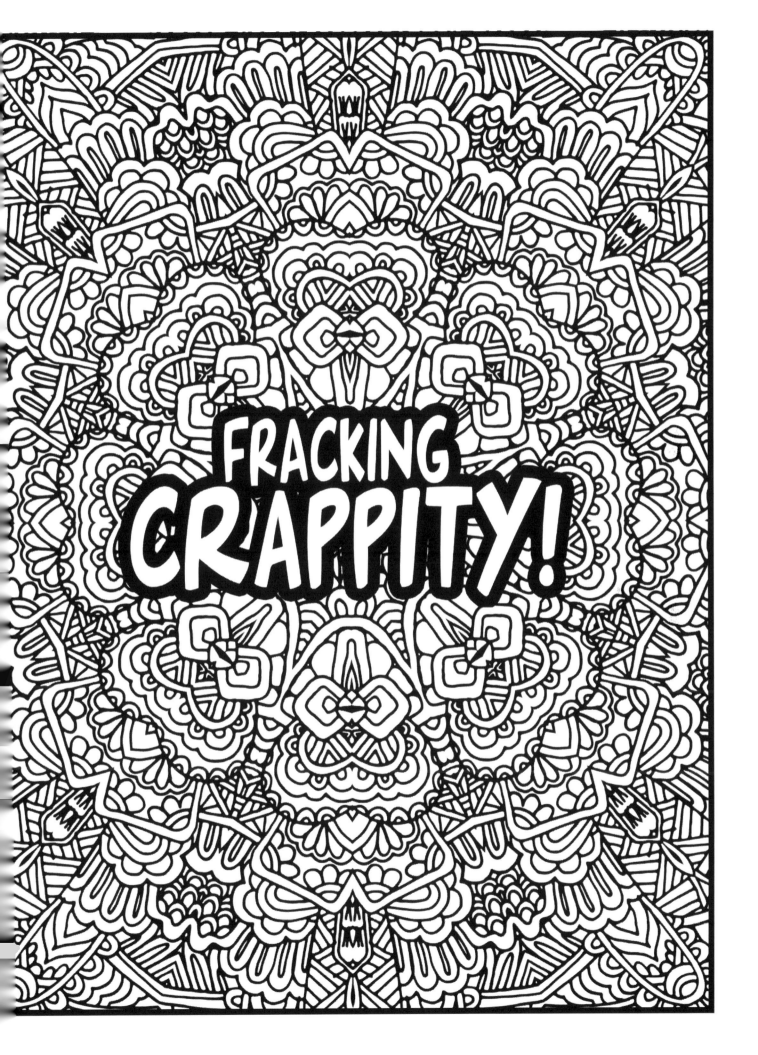

BSM CUSCOLO. Publising

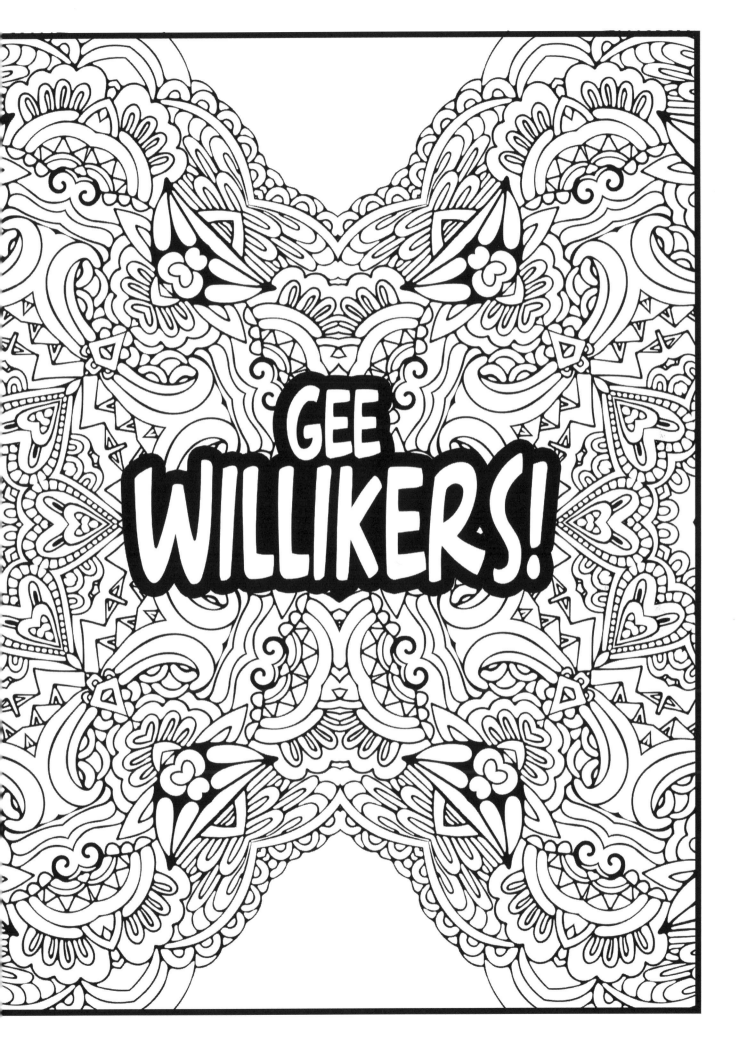

BSM CUSCOLO. Publising

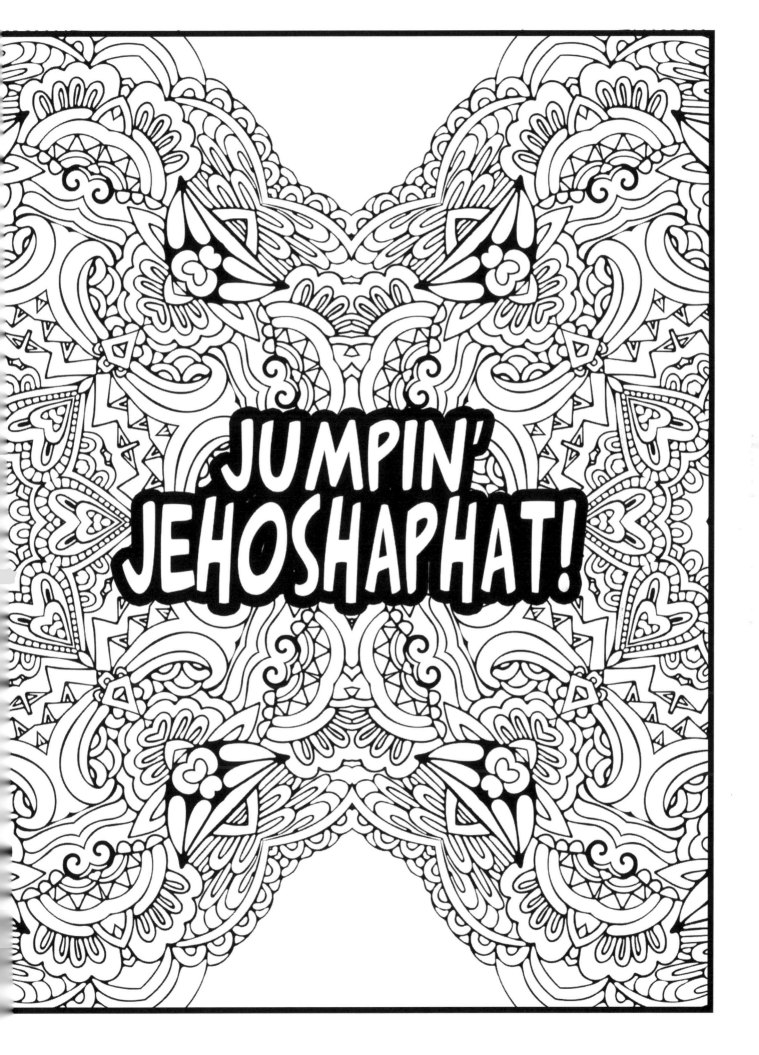

BSM CUSCOLQ. Publising

BSM CUSCOLO. Publising

BSM CUSCOLO.
Publising

BSM CUSCOLO.
Publising

BSM CUSCOLO.
Publising

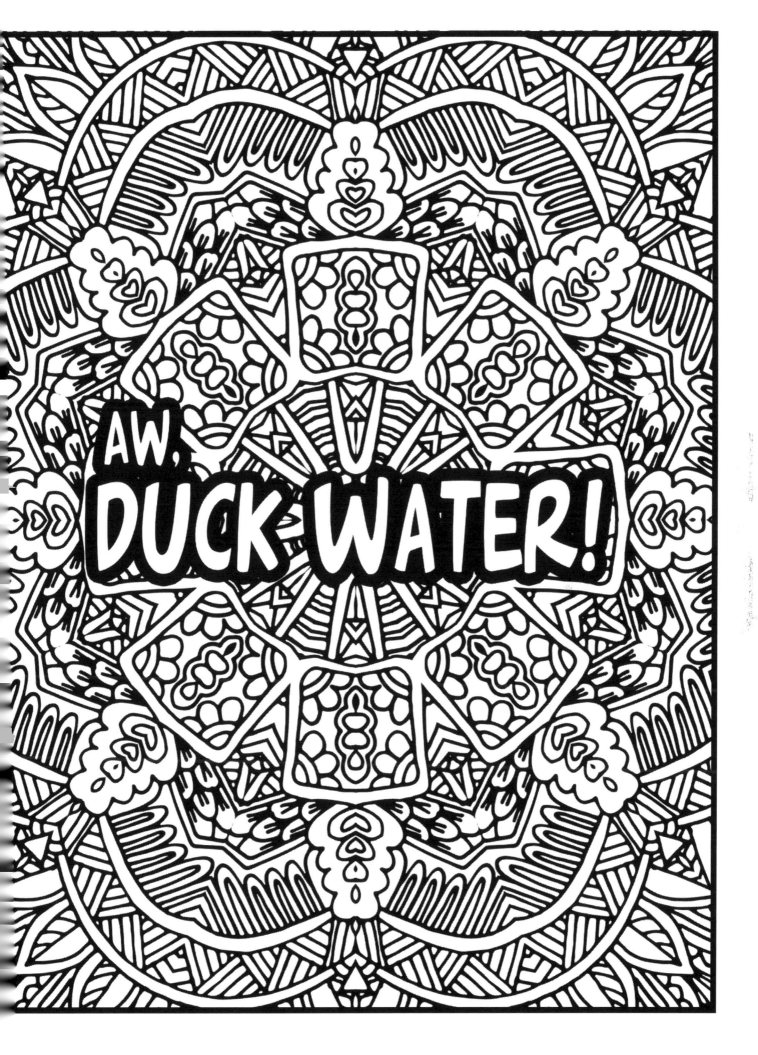

BSM CUSCOLO.
Publising

BSM CUSCOLO.
Publising

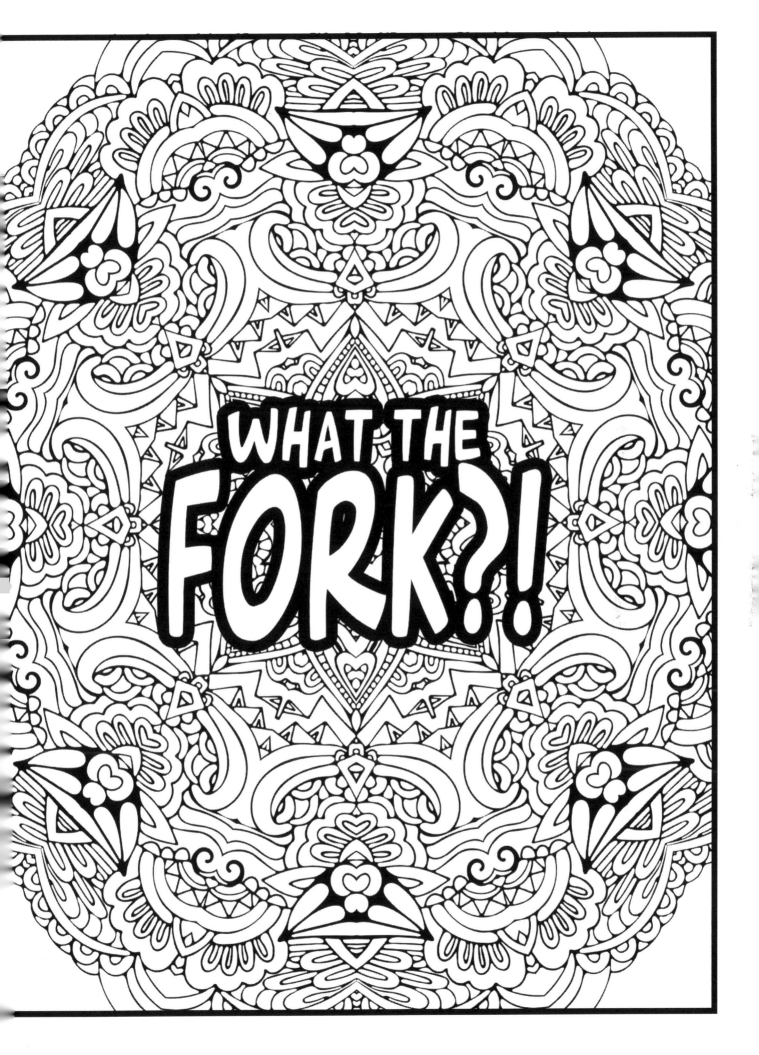

BSM CUSCOLO.
Publising

BSM CUSCOLO. Publising

" A GOOD REVIEW WILL REALLY HELP US KEEP IN THE HARD WORK "

★ ★ ★ ★ ★

thank you

Made in the USA
Monee, IL
30 November 2021